Peter Jäger

Outguard 27848

The WW II diary of German Private First Class
Paul Velte

Bibliographische Information der Deutschen Nationalbibliothek:
Die Deutsche Nationalbibliothek verzeichnet diese Publikation
In der Deutschen Nationalbibliographie; detaillierte bibliographische
Daten sind im Internet über http://dnb.dnb.de abrufbar.

© 2017 Peter Jäger
p.jaeger.metrologie@web.de
Herstellung und Verlag:
BoD – Books on Demand, Norderstedt

ISBN: 978-3-7431-6211-2

Acknowledgments

I would like to thank my friend Mark Grantham for his kind assistance in helping me to prepare this book in English language. I made him volunteer to do all necessary corrections. Read what Mark wrote when he had finished his work:

"Hi Peter,
Thank you for allowing me to do this for you. It is a great honor to learn about your uncle and how he did such brave things for his fellow soldiers/friends and for the protection of his home and family during WWII. The likes of his Generation, I fear, will never be seen again on this Earth. Hopefully, we will also never see a war again like he went through. "

Thank You!!

Hey Mark: Air Force rocks!

But most of all I want to thank my wife Petra. It was her idea to publish this book in English language. Petra, I love you.

Table of Contents

Acknowledgments 5
Prologue 7
The Diary 9
Thoughts about the campaign against Russia 74
Notifications to Pauls familiy 82
Acronyms and Abbreviations 100
Names and Persons 101

Prologue

The origin of the diary you hold in your hands was a gift of my 75 year old aunt Elsa in the mid 90's.
It was written by her brother in WWII with a now fading pencil in a kind of old German sutterlin style. So, I decided to type it to be able to read it fluently.

The story was so fascinating that I decided to publish and share it after my aunts death in 2015.
The diary covers the last few months my uncle was alive before he was killed at age 24 as a soldier in Russia.

The diary covers a small part of WW II from a different point of view what most articles report about the war and Hitler's strategies. It's the point of view of a young PFC with all the worries and thoughts most soldiers had in the unknown and strange situation of a war:
- Who is the new commander?
- How is the food
- Where will I sleep tonight?

The soldiers were excited about mail from home. Some dark thoughts came up when holidays arrived – everybody wanted to be home at Easter or other holidays, thinking of family and great food.

In everyday life, Paul's focus was not on the war itself or possible death.
However, this subject is discussed, e.g. in the section "*Thoughts about the campaign against Russia*", it can be seen how intensively one was dealing with this topic.

Remarkable is how accurate Paul's unit took care about him after his death. All belongings - from socks to chewing gum and cigarettes – were listed and sent back home.
The company commander as well as comrades wrote letters – handwritten or with typewriter.

The printed diary hasn't been changed regarding structure, style and if possible spelling and punctuation to keep it as authentic as possible.

To complete the story, photos and documents were added to the diary.
The photos were arranged on separate pages because the diary itself doesn't have any photos at all.

Remember: Paul hasn't had a cell phone, internet or a daily paper – the information he had was the information he was given!

The Diary

Diary

German Private First Class

Paul Velte

O.U., may 25th 1941

Today, it's may 25th, 1941.

I decided to write a diary. The time we are living in made me make that decision.

Since march 31st we are on our way, starting from Eichstadt, where our quarters for the winter have been. So many thoughts about what was coming up and where we might be sent to.

So many rumors came up – none became real. Just for that reason – not knowing what will happen and how will it end – in other words I feel absolutely gloomy about my future in this stressful time – I decided to keep track and write this diary.

In case something happens to me in the upcoming campaign I kindly ask the finder of this diary to send it to my parents, who live under the following address:

Family
Paul Velte
Remscheid-Hasten
Ludendorffstr. 34

I will try now to catch up with the time from march 31st until today.
I will pick out just the interesting days only to prevent boring someone by reading unimportant facts.

March 31, 1941, 5.00 o'clock in the morning. Pouring rain outside. The engines of our Henschels, which haven't been used all winter long are warming up, idling. Today is the day, the beginning of our trip with unknown destiny. It's said we go to Posen. There we shall be shipped. Where to is hidden in the dark. Orders for departure came, the trucks pull out.

I am driving with the third group, just our sergeant has changed. The new one is Sergeant Stephan, same age. My co-driver is Heinz Pieper. In Warthbrücken we pick up another 2 guys of our company, then we go ahead. In the meantime the sunshine broke through, but it's still raining- Just before Posen we make a right turn. We proceed to a small village named Ohrendorf.

The company rests in a school building. We drivers stay in a farmhouse. We are really astonished and impressed by the immense troop movements that just take place.

April 3rd, 1941
We arrive at Camp Warthe A huge troop training camp near Posen. Rumors say there's an exercise. Nobody knows how long we will stay here.

April 5 and 6, 1941
There's a huge exercise going on; with 47 Generals around. Most guns are tested, they are called D0 guns. The batteries shoot over our heads, we have never experienced anything like that. The air is thunder, the earth is shaking caused by impact after impact.

April 8, 1941
Orders out of the blue. We had to cut loading blocks. Again all we could do is just guess where they will send us to. Some say we will head south, because trouble has started down there.

Others claim we proceed further to the east. But that doesn't make any sense. We make the short distance to the border to get embarked.

April 11, 1941
Wake up call at 01.30 o'clock. At 02.30 the vehicles are ready. Ride to the Posen Railway station. Finally, at 11.00 o'clock we get embarked. Like so often we get our job done without any problems. The weather is great, just a little chilly. At 13.00 o'clock the train starts moving.

von Posen. Wir liegen in Baracken. Ich habe gehört dass eine grosse Übung stattfinden. Wie lange wir hier liegen bleiben sollen wissen wir nicht.

5.+6 April. Es ist eine grosse Übung im Gange, im beisein von 47 Generäle. Es werden die neusten Geschütze ausprobiert, man nennt sie Pr Geschütze. Die Arie schiesst über uns weg, so was haben wir noch nicht gehört. Die Luft ist von einem dröhnen erfüllt. Aufschlag auf Aufschlag erschüttert die Erde.

8. April. Ein Blitz wie aus heiterem Himmel. Verladeklötze schneiden. Jetzt kommt wie so oft das grosse Rätselraten, wo geht es hin. Verschiedene behaupten wir kommen zum Süden. Denn da unten hat angefangen zu knallen. Andere wieder behaupten, es geht weiter zum Osten. Aber das will keinem einleuchten. Die kurze Strecke bis zur Grenze und dann verladen.

11 April. 1:30 Uhr ist schon wecken. 2:30

Original script of diary's opposite page

April 12, 1941

I woke up at 07.00 o'clock. First of all I try to figure out where we are. We just pass Warsaw. I need to think about the victory parade after the campaign against Poland. Full of pride we passed the Führer. Meanwhile we've heard from some railway workers that we have to leave the train in Sidlce, funny name – better we say Slice. We arrive at 13.00 o'clock. My truck left the the train first.

They put us in a school building. A real bughole. We work late to get the rooms clean. We have caught about 20 bugs. All the beds need to be washed off with gasoline to get rid of the bugs. And tomorrow we'll celebrate Easter!

April 13, 1941 Easter

Today I have to deliver coal and straw to the battalion in pouring rain. Guess I will remember this Easter for a long time!

PFC Paul Velte

April 18, 1941
We shall move again. They want us to move back. They are talking about a two day exercise. About 160 km to our next quarters. The ride starts at 13.00 o'clock. We're all in a great mood in my driver's cab., We've all received Easter packages from home. Even late these boxes brought me into Easter holiday mood.
We spend the night in a barn.

April 19, 1941
11.00 o'clock we start and drive all the way through to the new camp. On my way I had two flat tires that needed to be changed. At 22.00 o'clock we arrive at our quarters in Pulaweg on the river Vistula. We are really surprised: We reach a big and brand new base.
But when I think about the base life with all the duties I am kind of scared. For more than two years I'm all around these places and now they put me back to bootcamp? Can't imagine that.

April 22, 1941
Have to bring newsfiles to a place called Pionki near Radom. All the way miserable roads and critical weather conditions. A distance of 150 km (100 miles) at a speed of 25 km per hour (15 mph), you really need iron nerves to get through that, but after almost three years in the military you get used to such.

April 27, 1941
For the first time ever I'm on guard. Person in charge is Sergeant Stephan. But everything works fine. Today some guys returned from days off.

April 28, 1941
This morning the division commander showed up. My report worked fine, everything worked fine today.

May 07, 1941
Today the vehicles will be mustered. I've got a new radiator for my truck. The inspection went well. Result: ok!
I've gotten used to the life in a military base, thanks to our protecting first sergeant.

May 13, 1941
Today we had to load the trucks. It appears we will leave soon. Sooner than expected! This afternoon I'm on guard again.

May 15, 1941
Beautiful weather and we're heading east. Finally we arrive in a small village named Lobaczow, just next to the Russian border. We move into the barracks. What are all these troop movements for? That's the question, again. Rumors come up: Russia grants the German troops to proceed to the south without any attacks
Others say that's not true with Russia. The only thing I know is that there is a reason that we're here and it has never been such a secret.
All roads must be fixed and ready by may 25th and I need to say: we really did a job! The roads are in excellent conditions.

May 23, 1941
Today I have to go to a construction area. Our company is building lookout stands for observation posts. I've been on such a lookout stand. Right in front of me I could see the river Bug, which divides Poland and Russia. High up you see the Brest Fortress . Right on the opposite banks of the river Bug you can spot Russias observation nests.

May 24, 1941

With my platoon I went to a new camp in the woods, where we will move to in a few days
Some log cabins will be built. Nobody knows how long we will stay there.
The barracks we live in have to be emptied for comrades of the air defense units. There are so many troops all around this place – nobody knows where they are all from and where they will have to go.
Everywhere in the woods and all along the border are German soldiers. Don't tell me that doesn't mean anything! This afternoon a Russian fighter planes flew along the border.

May 25, 1941

Today is my writing day. Who knows what the future will bring us. Tomorrow we'll proceed to the camp in the woods. I'm scared to death thinking about all of these mosquitos.

May 26, 1941
This morning we proceeded to the new camp. But we didn't move into the camp in the woods. Location is great. A few kilometers ahead we can see the Russian observation posts.
We are obviously close to an airport. Every now and then Russian aircraft are in the air. The weather is great. I think the temperature is about 80 degrees. For the first time this year we could take a swim outside.

May 27, 1941
Still fabulous weather. Installed a new carburetor.

May 29, 1941
There are free barracks near a village named Kowdczn, orders make us go there. Just ahead of us is artillery. 10,5 cm guns. They are well covered, facing the frontier.

May 30, 1941
We made log mats for the vehicles. Nothing new.

May 31, 1941
The company has to build a new emergency bridge. Today the rumor spread that Ribbentrop is in Moscow. I have no idea if this is true or not. Tomorrow is Pentecost. How long will we stay here. Air defense made tactical changes of position.
I'm questioning myself do we really just march through Russia. More and more I'm in doubt. I don't believe anything anymore except there'll be a big bang soon. I feel healthy, just the damn mosquitos, really bad. Guess the close by swamp is the reason. All my body is covered with bites, itching like crazy.
Last week it was said after Pentecost we'll know more, but still nothing. Looks like we're gonna stay here for another two weeks. But what are 14 days of waiting and staying when in the end nothing goes on fast enough.

June 01st, 1941 (Pentecost)
A great Pentecost day, outstanding weather. Took a sunbath today. We didn't receive any better news today. Now I'll write a letter home. Yesterday I received a letter from Mum and Elsa.

June 13, 1941
I haven't written for a few days, always the same. Been to the construction area a few times, they are binding fascines, for the swamp roads.
Flossachferries are built, all ahead of time. Mölders is here in our section, as well as the Richthofen fighter wing. Today I've heard that Italian fighter planes have arrived in our section Propably the result of the meeting between Führer - Duce, at the Brenner mountain.
Last night I've been on night guard between 12.00 - 02.00 o'clock. Indescribable seeing all the troops still moving. More and more troops are moved in together, right here next to the border. Soldiers are wherever you go and everybody strongly believes there's an upcoming combat against Russia, against Bolshevism.
This morning the first reconnaissance airplane, a Fokke-Wulf, an aircraft with double fuselage, flew over our heads. Above the border it made a turn and flew the same route again. Immediately three Russian fighters were up in the air.
This afternoon a German reconnaissance airplane showed up once in a while and patrolled the border. Our battalion was strengthened by an additional company.
The battle against Russia comes close. But why war against Russia? That's my question. Propably exactly what I imagine myself.

In Russia they have Bolshevism, just the pure opposite of our idea. In one of his speeches the Führer talked about a Reorientation of Europe.
This requires a change of the system of the Russian government, yes, the complete destruction of Bolshevism.
But there is no way they will just give up their system without opposition. Russia will try now to give everyone weapons and set up an army that will, if we are not very observant, destroy us and start fighting before we get aware of that.
For that reason we will not rest until this enemy, world's enemy No. 1 is on the ground and completely destroyed.

June 15, 1941
Another sunday without any time for my own. This morning we drivers had to load the trucks, with fascines and logs for ferries. At noon they said we will move out today. So we loaded our personal belongings, too. At 22.00 o'clock we start, heading for our new quarters, right on the border. Word say that the war will start in with four waves. What a great future. It's said that we have a very bad section for an attack. I say any attack must be very unexpected, so the enemy has no time to think about the defense. I am sure it all will work.

June 15, 1941
We've spent the first night in our new quarters. We are dislocated in different barns. 500 meters ahead is the river Bug. This name will be in everybody's mouth in a short time.
The day went quietly. Yesterday I've received a letter from an unknown girl Gerda Klever. Wrote her back today. I can imagine where she's got my address from. Guess my sister Elsa is involved.

June 18, 1941
Since the early morning hours polish refugees are passing us heading west. Terespol, the town we are close by will be cleaned and emptied. As soon as the Polish rested down we had to make them move again. Again, primitive trucks on the road try to find their way into an unknown future. Many won't find their houses again. You back home, thank god that he protects you from a war in your own country. A few british aircraft dropping bombs in the night are no big deal compared to this. Thousands and thousands will lose their homes and everything they have here very soon.

June 19, 1941
Troops are still moving all around us. A never ending column traffic arrives at the border.
Today, we pulled back our vehicles into foxholes. The woods are full of troops. The world hasn't seen an attack like this.

June 20, 1941
We dug shelter trenches today. Always two men per hole. How many days are left until the biggest show ever. It has to be soon.
Until tomorrow evening, 19:00 o'clock any coming traffic will be stopped on the roads planned for the attack.
Tomorrow, the company will go into position. How many of my comrades I will never see again next week. Probably I might be missing, too, who knows. Back home they won't believe that the war in the east started again, but this time against such an mighty enemy. Back home, they don't know about all the preparations that are going on here, probably they just assume.
But they definitely cannot assume that we all are so close to such an important decision.

Paul in Remscheid, at his parents house in Ludendorffstraße 34, today's Büchelstraße 34. The building still exists.

June 21, 1941, in the evening at 21:00 o'clock
The last preparations are made. Our chief spoke to us this afternoon. At 03:00 o'clock this night the first shot will fall on our side. The inevitable seems our destiny. Will it turn out good? Let's hope. Just in case something happens to me: best wishes to all of you. Your thankful son Paul.

June 22, 1941, in the morning at 03:15 o'clock
I get out of my sleep, need to collect my thoughts. First I think of thunder and lightning but soon I see clearly. The campaign In the east has begun. Heavy artillery fires its doom against our enemy. Like the end of the world the air is filled with hiss and thunder of the D0 guns. This scary weapon I already wrote about (see camp Warthe).
Immediately German fighter aircraft and StuKas are thundering over our heads. Fighters are chasing low level against the enemy. StuKas rush down almost perpendicular towards their targets. The airport I wrote about already is burning in flames.
Two hostile aircrafts can make it up in the air from the destroyed ground but understand soon that our fighters are superior.
Dr. Goebbels announces a Führers proclamation. Now we know why the Führer lets the weapons talk. Then Ribbentrop speaks.

Absolutely squalid what the Russians have done. All our hate breaks through against the world's enemy No. 1. Now they will get what they've asked for.

Russian bombers fly above our heads, a large number of aircraft.

Two are immediately taken down by our FlaK. We can hear the other aircraft's dropped bombs exploding. Then they come back, chased by German fighter aircraft. Men from the Mölders squadron. Air combat like I have seen in Poland in the West campaign is going on. It's terribly beautiful watching them crashing down one after another. Not a single hostile fighter returns to its home base.

Our first sergeant returns and tells us the news. Brest is fallen at 09:00 o'clock, just a small citadel still resists. Our division has as good as no loss. Russia couldn't stand an attack like the one we made this morning. The moment I'm writing this another 30 StuKas lift off heading against the enemy. Up to now the radio didn't spread any news about the fights. It's 20:00 o'clock. During the afternoon another 5 or 6 hostile aircraft were shot down. One wreck lies close to our position. The tail gunner's body is charcoaled. When crashing down the bombardier released his bombs und set some houses on fire. At 18:00 o'clock the first prisoners came passing by. Weird figures you haven't even seen from Poland.

They all have already torn off the soviet star. Many don't even wear uniforms. Some are just in underwear or sportswear. A sign that they've been completely surprised. There are Mongols, Chinese, Tibetans and Jews among the prisoners. A sad picture that we see. A picture of misery.

That's how the first day of the campaign against Russia ends. May we continue to be fortunate.

June 23, 1941
At 16:00 o'clock we left our shelter and drove to our company. In the dark we proceed over the river Bug to Iwachnowice. A 40 km drive. We take up quarters in that village.

June 24, 1941
In the afternoon we continue to proceed. On our way our fighters shot down 5 hostile aircraft. The runway has been invaded by another division. We need to take tracks across the fields. Sand and more sand. Pretty often the trucks appear to get stuck. It grew dark. You don't see anything due to all the dust.

We take a rest until sunrise – in road trenches, like so often.

The Soviets have deported former Polish people, who don't agree with the Russian government to Siberia.

This week, another 10 men shall be abducted from another village. Really Bolshevik. The Polish are glad that the Germans came.

June 25, 1941
At dawn we proceed through the desert sands of Russia. We are part of an advance detachment now. Guderians tanks are further ahead. Gas, food and ammunition are transported by JU 52.
The tanks are 150 km ahead of us. On our way we've built a bridge and kept on proceeding. We made 130 km this day.

June 26, 1941
Heading towards the front together with our assault artillery.! Our company is part of an advance detachment. Since 05:00 o'clock we are ready for action. Finally, at 11:00 we start. Ahead of us heavy assault guns on the road, followed by a PAK detachment. Behind the motorcycle riflemen we are with our Henschel. Additionally there are bicycle troops and cavalry troops, too.
Task is to encircle and close down Bialystock. The population is exited. Wherever we stop they bring milk. They tell us about the suppression by the Russians.

They had to work four long days for just 2 pounds of bacon. Again and again the people complain about how they were sucked out. On the run, the Russians set fire to villages. The cavalry squadron has broken local resistance and has captured 10 prisoners. The path through the sand and swamp is inexorable. The vehicles have to give up what they can. At 1:00 o'clock in the night our daily destination is reached. I'm so tired – I'm just about to drop. We've made 83 Kilometers today. The village we came to is called Zegorowice.

June 27, 1941
At 05.00 clock they already woke us up again, then we pack our things and get ready to depart. Our company had to search the place for Russian soldiers this morning. We found a Russian army ration supply depot, which will help us through the next days. At 13:00 o'clock our section is commissioned to search the site outside the village for Russians. I have to accompany them with my truck. In a village I stay back while my group deploys. The village girls and women decorate my truck with flowers.

The truck never ever looked like this before. We made 8 prisoners, which need to be brought back. There is the highest alertness level for us and we have to return to the company. The Russians plan a break through. Our company is in position. Finally 3 were wounded. Lt Pfeifer, PFC Wächter and one other guy of our company.

June 28, 1941
The night was pretty quiet. In the morning we've received the news that Hans Wächter passed away caused by his injuries. The first grave on enemy's territory. A tank attack has been repulsed. The circle around 2 tank divisions and 5 infantry Divisions has been closed. This evening our company has been relieved and is coming back.

June 29, 1941
We're going back to our battalion, a 52 Kilometer distance. Snipers are hell of a problem. Again and again German soldiers get killed behind the front line.

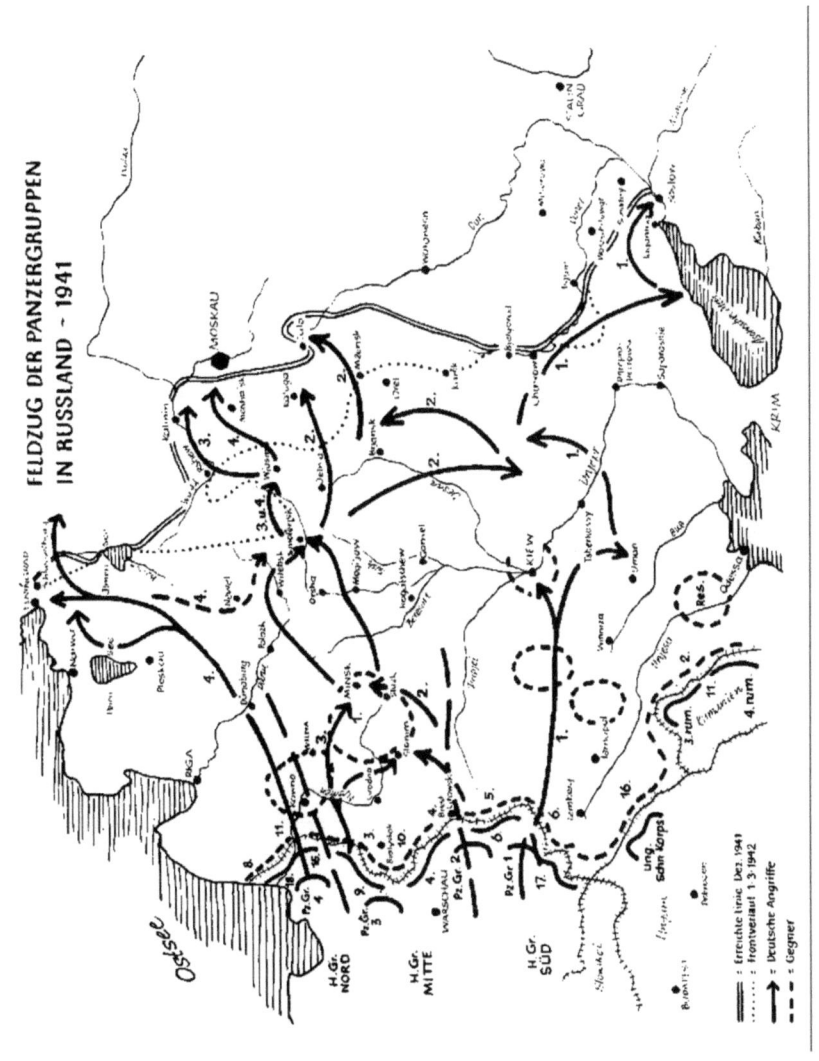

June 30, 1941
Between front. This afternoon we've received orders to place mines. First platoon had to go on its own. After a 26 kilometer drive along the front line we reached our destination. The mines shall be actually placed by infantry pioneers. We drive back. It's become dark meanwhile. The truck with the trailer that was used to transport the mines received engine damage. I had to take over the trailer. Everywhere around us gunfire by Russian soldiers hidden in the woods. On our way we went through some very exciting minutes. German antitank guns and air defense guns shot over our heads so close, that the bullets ware just above the truck. We answered with a signal rocket and they shot at a higher angle,
At 01:00 o'clock at night we arrived at our quarters.

July 1st, 1941
Great weather, as always. We had a calm day today, but one of my tires went flat. Company platoon went out for reconnaissance. Hopefully we won't need it tonight. Nobody thinks about what it means to be on these roads at night in sand and dust. Besides that a quiet day.

July 2nd, 1941
As I had guessed it happened. Last night we had to depart and drive back to the former place to Zeyowice. We drove all night. It should have started at 5:00 o'clock – but as late as 13:00 o'clock we received the march orders. Again we are with the advance detachment. Another 35 kilometers to go. Spent the night in In a small village. On the road are tanks next to tanks next to tanks. Hundreds of vehicles are left destroyed in the road ditch … .

July 3rd, 1941
Today's mothers birthday. Thought about it this morning when I woke up and send her all luck from here from enemy territory.
We made about 30 kilometers and stay in a small village, resting. Today and tomorrow we can rest . Really close there's a field airdrome.
German bombs are dropped without a break and against the enemy, who are on the run again. Weather is still beautiful, and I feel great, like the weather.
It's getting dark and I need to prepare my sleeping cabin. This place is, as in previous two campaigns, the cab of my truck. They wake us up as late as 08:00 o'clock. The last days were really hard. Day and night behind the wheel, lack of sleep, nobody can take that.

July 4, 1941
The 3rd group and me and my truck have to get out and fix a small bridge.

July 5, 1941
Departure right over the runway, heading for Nieswicz. At 18 o'clock the company had to muster. Seven men were awarded with E.K.2 . We proceed at 18:30 o'clock. At 20 o'clock we cross the border Poland / Russia. At 24 o'clock at midnight we finally reach at our quarters. A 60 km ride.

July 6, 1941
We proceed from noon on. Another emergency bridge had to be fixed. First platoon went on its own. At 20:00 o'clock the bridge is fixed and we get back on the road. We pass by a bigger town. There we get 15 boxes of butter, about 7 ½ Zentner (750 lbs). Back on the road we have to get through a dead abates. This abates is about 30 meters long and 10 meters wide. At 12 o'clock we finally get some sleep.

July 7, 1941
The company follows but meets some leftover Russian troops. Complain 3 dead and 3 wounded. Wake up call at 2.30 o'clock and back on the road. At 15:00 o'clock we finally meet the company. At 18 o'clock we proceed to Zank, spend the night there.

July 8, 1941
Wake up call at 3.30 o'clock. We proceed using tank tracks. On our way prisoners are made. Arrive at our todays destination early. Can rest there.

July 9, 1941
We depart at 13.00 o'clock. Road is miserable. Same parts have to be repaired first. Again we are in a swamp. We spend the night in a farmhouse. A night to go crazy. Thousands and thousands of mosquitos are humming through the air like StuKas. Can't even think about getting sleep.

July 10, 1941
Wake up at 2.30 o'clock. My head feels squared caused by all the mosquito bites. Hands and feet are itching like crazy. It never has been that bad.
At 03:15 o'clock the 3rd Platoon leaves. The roads and bridges need to be fixed, again.
At the Beresina, we take quarters. In the afternoon we're fixing roads again. Pulled as much as 5 stranded trucks out of the sand with my truck.

July 11, 1941
At 5.45 o'clock we are torn from sleep by a Russian aircraft. It dropped bombs real close to us.
First platoon builds a Flossack ferry until 11 o'clock. I have to accompany them with my truck.
In the afternoon the 2nd platoon ferries cavalry troops of our advance detachment across. Leisure time for us.

July 12, 1941
Wake up call at 5 o'clock. At 8 o'clock we make it over a war bridge stretching over the river Beresina. Around noon we are in our new post.

July 13, 1941
At 2.00 o'clock they woke up 1st platoon; they have to repair roads for the proceeding troops. It's the worst road we were on yet. Again, at noon we are at our new destination.

July 14, 1941
Wake up at 3.00 o'clock. At 4 o'clock we're on the road, heading towards the new post. Company must build an emergency bridge across the river Rhiet. We drivers do the security detachment with machine guns. At 20 o'clock 2. Pi 31 und 3. Pi 34 take over.

July 15, 1941
Finally slept 8 hours. 1st platoon has to fix roads. A Fieseler Storch aircraft dropped important information for our detachment. Therefore we departed at 20.30 o'clock across the river Rhiet to a village. 1st platoon secures us with 4 heavy anti tank guns.

July 16, 1941
At 5.00 o'clock we proceed. Road is pretty good. At 15 o'clock we arrive at a war airfield. At 18 o'clock Russian aircraft try to attack the airfield.

Due to great air defense they quit. Immediately our fighter aircraft are up in the air, Mölders is among them. His plane can be easily spotted by its black wings. Mölders shoots down another 5 Russian planes. This morning he received diamonds to his Knight's Cross. So far he has shot down as many as 105 hostile aircraft.

July 17, 1941
1.30 o'clock to the front, to the meat can on the Dnieper. The Stalin line is still here, but soon the enemy is encircled. At 3.30 we drive into position. But immediately 6 red aircraft are above us. Heading towards the airfield. Dropping bombs, trying to escape. But like the day before our aircraft are behind them, chasing them. One after another drops down to earth like a burning torch. One of the aircraft completely explodes in the air. Mölders shot down another two again.

First platoon goes into position. Wolga-German deserters come over and fight with us. We will keep some of them as translators. They depict the conditions which prevail among the Soviets and are glad that they are with us.

July 18, 1941
I could sleep a little longer today and got up at 10 o'clock. Really close are three batteries of artillery. At 16:00 o'clock the Russians attack. Enemy artillery aims at our positions. But immediately our guns start its drums. The attack is thrown back, many prisoners are made. The enemy artillery tries to shoot at our batteries, so we are enclosed by enemy fire. The Russians shoot wild with no success. Just during the fire I receive mail. Two letters from Gerda Klever and two parcels from aunt Auguste. Yes, the cigarette is great now to calm down in this situation. The company is relieved by infantry and we drive back some kilometers. Reconnaissance reports that the Russians set up 40 batteries – this is 160 heavy guns.

July 19, 1941
Had to drive back to Brgcow last night. This morning they woke us up at 06:00 o'clock. Departure at 07.40 o'clock. Need to get covered at St. Brgcow suburbans. Division after division are marching through. From the left a whole Regiment appears. Around 03.00 o'clock we drive south to a small village. Company goes into position. Wrote a letter home, it's almost early morning.

July 20, 1941

Departure at 06:00 o'clock. Today was an important day for our advance detachment. The order: shut the box – close the meat can.

The roads were almost impassable. We went over railway tracks, rails, sand and through forests where our truck almost couldn`t make it through. Two combat patrols with antitank guns, our company moves forward. At 11:00 o'clock the attack starts. The Russian artillery has established itself. But immediately our fighter aircraft are up in the air and drives them out of their holes.

The enemy moves back and we march into the village without loosing any time. Antitank guns and two 15 cm guns move into position.

Infantry regiment 12 I.R. 12 maneuver closer and proceeds. Soon a battery of mobile air defense guns enhances the scene. A combat patrol got hold of a complete battery of 15 cm howitzers with their gunners and now they shoot at their own folks

The second combat patrol destroyed as much as six tanks. One tank was blown up by Eule Domhöfer with a hand grenade.

In the afternoon our advance detachment broke through the Russian front, from all units we are furthest ahead. With that break through seven trucks with ammunition were destroyed and one tank.

200 to 300 prisoners were made. Our own losses are four men of an antitank gun platoon, they drove on a mine. From our company two more men died who were wounded on july 7 .

July 21, 1941
This morning another reconnaissance patrol left. Straight 200 meters ahead is a battery of 15 cm guns in position. The Russian artillery tries to destroy our battery. They miss, but their grenades explode really close. The reconnaissance patrol found more than 150 mines and has to find a path through that mine field.
In the early evening we built foxholes to protect against shrapnel. Then we go to sleep. Our 15 cm battery destroyed three of the enemy's batteries.
I.R. 82 took 2500 prisoners yesterday.

July 22, 1941
We got up at 07:00 o'clock. Around us everybody is firing. The 2. Infantry battalion proceeded over the river Dnjepr. For the very first time I see a Russian fighter plane, a monoplane, which flies low level over our heads. We drivers are the covering party this night.

July 23, 1941
I've already made an oil change at 07.00 o'clock. At 10 o'clock the 1st platoon departs, together with a cavalry section, a bicycle platoon and an anti tank gun. Now we are part of „Hürten" blocking command.
Left and right of the road we search the woods, looking for Russians. Some prisoners were taken. Three bridges have been blown up and need to be replaced. A Russian Martin bomber comes flying over our heads but doesn't attack. Around 09:00 o'clock we arrive at our destination.
We take rest in a Collective farm. A complete platoon with passenger cars got stuck in a swamp and I received orders to go and pull them out. On my way I drove over a Russian mine. It didn't explode – lucky me!

July 24, 1941
Wake up call at 07:00 o'clock. The weather is a little better now. For the first time in a week the sun is shining. A mine locating platoon swarms out, looking for mines and disarm them. You can clearly see the tire tracks of my truck crossing a mine – and in exactly that mine the fuze didn't work.
At 11 o'clock the company comes after. We rest the remaining day. In the distance a thunderstorm is coming up. The sun is burning down like crazy. Groups 2. + 3. have to get out again. Placing and securing mines.

July 25, 1941
Last night at 11.00 o'clock they woke us up. Alert! A reconnaissance patrol leaves. At 02.30 o'clock I pick up the group and the mines. We follow the company, which has left already. The orders: take the city of Bugaczew in a surprise raid. The Russians obviously expected our attack and are in position.
The Russians welcome us with heavy artillery fire we haven't experienced before. Our commander gets wounded and was brought back. All available weapons are in position. The enemy's fire is unbelievable and scary. The bicycle squadron lost 32 men. An air defense gun and all the men were completely destroyed. Our 2nd platoon has two men down and another two wounded.
The vehicles were ordered back. At 06.00 o'clock the 152. Division releases us, we return to the previous place to rest.

July 26, 1941
Wake up call at 07.00 o'clock. IT's quiet around us. In the distance we can hear grenades' thunder.
The supply of the Russians over Bergaczew has been cut off this morning. It will not be long and this meat can is finished. This meat can is located exactly where the river Drut unites with the River Diyeps.

July 27, 1941
Lieutenant Prahl takes over the command of our company. Our group has to repair roads.

July 28, 1941
Fixing roads, like the day before. Group 1. And 2. Places mines. Bombers circle above Rogatschew and attack important targets.

July 29, 1941
Had to replace the 3. Platoon, they needed to wash and shower. At 14:00 o'clock we were released again. Last night, the Russians shot harassing fire with long-range artillery. D0 guns from our side.

July 30, 1941
We took a bath in the river Drut today. The day was hot. A heat to collapse and flies and nothing but flies. While there were the mosquitos in the Rokitno swamps who drove us crazy it's the flies here.

July 31, 1941
We've been taking a swim for 4 hours this morning. Our previous advance detachment was put together again, under the command of captain Brinkmann. Motorcycle riflemen, anti tank guns and reconnaissance are already here. Okay, the race can start.

August 1, 1941
In the front line, S + T mines are laid and secured.

August 2, 1941
Lock and secure, like the previous day.

August 3, 1941
We are relieved by the Pi. 152, tomorrow the journey continues.

August 4, 1941
A distance of 80 km to go. Near Stari Biczow we cross the river Diyepi and take the runway to Ussochsi. We take quarters in a forest.

August 5, 1941
From up here the main attack is to take place. Our division is in reserve until the attack is over, then we shall follow the enemy.

August 6, 1941
Our new commander will be introduced. Nothing new. 1st Lt Dütting.

August 7, 1941
In the morning we went for a swim again. At noon we had to repair a road, which can be seen by the enemy. But an upcoming thunderstorm prevents to be seen. We receive the message that we return to the old place to continue defending the front section. The thunderstorm brings a lot of rain. A ride to go crazy. The roads are softened and aggravate driving.
The Russians, who attempted to destroy the Dujepi Bridge, were shot and then hung up on the old bridge as a deterrent to the population. 10.00 in the evening we get stuck on the track. Impossible to go on driving.

August 8, 1941

At dawn we proceed. It is still raining. At 09.00 o'clock we arrive at the old place. 4 vehicles got stuck on the bad and softened road and are coming in by and by. The 152 pi. is replaced.

August 9, 1941

Our task is to block and secure the intersection of the north + the west Front, and defend to the outmost when the Russians should try to break out. We are a blockbuster, Colonel Jordan and us have a lock section of 50 km. So a very thin personnel coverage.

August 10, 1941

Again, blocks are set up. It is almost impossible to break through here. We have had three losses so far caused by our own mines.

August 12, 1941

Each and every morning, dead or wounded Russians are in the locks. Mostly members of reconnaissance groups. The effect of the S-mines is terrible.

August 13, 1941

The weather has improved, the attack continues on all fronts. We lost our divisional commander. The Russians retreat slowly. The Russian line, which is opposite from us, is further fortified.

August 14, 1941

In Gomel, south of Rogachev, troop movements have been observed. It is noted that freight trains arrive and unload troops. Great food for our stukas. Since early this morning, 4 o'clock attacking wings of dive bombers are over our heads. The time now is 20.00 o'clock. Just another wave of 28 Stukas "Ju. 87"and 12 heavy bombers with fighter escorts bring iron rations to the Soviets for dinner.

The weather is great, and as I feel as well. It's getting dark early in the evenings. At 20.00 o'clock it starts to become dawn. At 3 o'clock, however, it is already bright again. The nights are very cool. It will not be long before we get snow on the fur.

August 15, 1941
Did not have to be on guard last night, so I slept well. We're still blocking. The barriers stretch through the woods for kilometers. Whoever wants to get through there must have a lot of luck. A few days ago, Sergeant Stephan, my group leader, got wounded by an own booby trap, but can stay here. We just received the message that Rogaczew has been taken. The city we were supposed to take in a surprise raid three weeks ago. It took hard battles until the city was in our hands. The advance continues.

August 16, 1941
New orders. The mine fields have to be cleared. We are working on that since the early morning. I have to drive for group 2. and 3. . The mines have to be removed by tomorrow evening. But we already made it this evening and in addition to our mines we found 10 Russian mines and blew them up.

August 17, 1941
Today's Sunday. We're cleaning the mines. We're waiting for the order to leave. The squadron and the reconnaissance squadron are already leaving. Today I've prepared another great meal: Roasted potatoes, goulash and cucumber salad. As dessert apple compote with honey.

August 18, 1941
Had to be on guard from 5 - 7 o'clock and prepared our breakfast afterwards. Sour kidneys with apple sauce and thickened milk. The order to depart came in. The trip takes us via Now Bycow over the river Dujepeer to our battalion. Arrived at 17.00 o'clock.

August 19, 1941
Wake up call at 2 o'clock, we leave at 02.30. Orders: unknown. In the afternoon we arrive at our destination. The 1st platoon belongs to the advance detachment again from tomorrow on.

August 20, 1941
Wake up call at 12 o'clock, we leave at 12:30. On our way we pass the company which left last evening. The ride continues through heavy terrain. No German soldier has ever set foot on these grounds.
The population is on the streets, waving us welcome. Wherever we stop they bring us bread and meat. A sign that they are happy because we have freed them from the pressure of the Soviets. In a village we spend the night.

August 21, 1941
Wake up call at 02:15 o'clock. In the night a heavy thunderstorm came down. It is still foggy. 2:50 o'clock we leave. Once again through villages where people are on the streets despite the early hour. Always the same scene. In a city that the Russians have destroyed themselves, the company joins us. A statue of Stalin is torn down. On we go. A bridge is being rebuilt and the order is fulfilled at 7:00 o'clock. The ring is closed without being hit by enemy resistance.

August 22, 1941
Wake up call at 07:00 o'clock, a group of scouts spread out. We are very astonished when we learn that in the meat bowl which we have made tight, there is no enemy at all. I think the Russians already exercise running for the next Olympics. At 19.00 o'clock we head back, the same way we came. At 21.00 o'clock we rest down and sleep.

August 23, 1941
At 03:00 clock our trip continues. On our way we received the news that our reconnaissance group drove on a mine. Sepp Wagner is dead, from the others we know nothing yet. In the morning hours we arrive at the river Sosch. Here, our divisional supplies couldn't proceed because the vehicles got stuck in the mud. A mound of several hundred meters must be laid. I drove wood all day. At about 16.00 o'clock the first vehicle rolls over the dam. Tomorrow some other places have to be improved.

August 24, 1941
Wake up call at 05:00 o'clock. We got back to work. Had to drive loads of wood like the previous day. Job is done by 15.00 o'clock, we're waiting for departure.

August 25, 1941
Have another day of rest. Our group, which had to repair something this afternoon, slaughtered 5 geese. The marching order comes through. Tomorrow morning 4 o'clock it starts. Probably a distance of 130 km to make.

August 26, 1941
We depart at 04:00 o'clock, same way back. Then we go ahead. Many divisions are moving forward. We pass Surash. At 21.00 o'clock we arrive at our today's destination. The last 50 km were miserable. On the whole, the distance we made today was 190 km.

August 27, 1941
We have quarters on a farm again. The farmers are sharing the livestock and fruit stock since this morning. Every peasant will be his own master again. The population is well-disposed towards us.

August 28, 1941
Another day of rest today. We are waiting for gasoline. Around noon comes the tanker and we continue a few kilometers. We belong to the 1. battalion of the 17th Infantry regiment now.

August 29, 1941

The 3rd group has to go with a group from the 2nd platoon for reconnaissance. The route is unknown, probably not yet free of enemy. Without any disturbance, we arrive at our destination. It is a small village. A commissioner and 2 Russian soldiers are captured. The company has already moved into the new quarters and we are going back there.

August 30, 1941

Today is Sunday. But not a lucky day for me. Platoon 1. + 3. have to build a small bridge. I have to drive wood again with my truck. With the first truckload already I got stuck in the mud up to the front axle. Must be pulled out. In the evening when I move off I have the same bad luck again. I drive over a small bridge and hardly I am over it, I hang up to the frame in the mud. A miserable mess, especially since ground water is still present. After 1 ½ hours I can finally free the car. Two Russian bombers were shot down by our fighter planes.

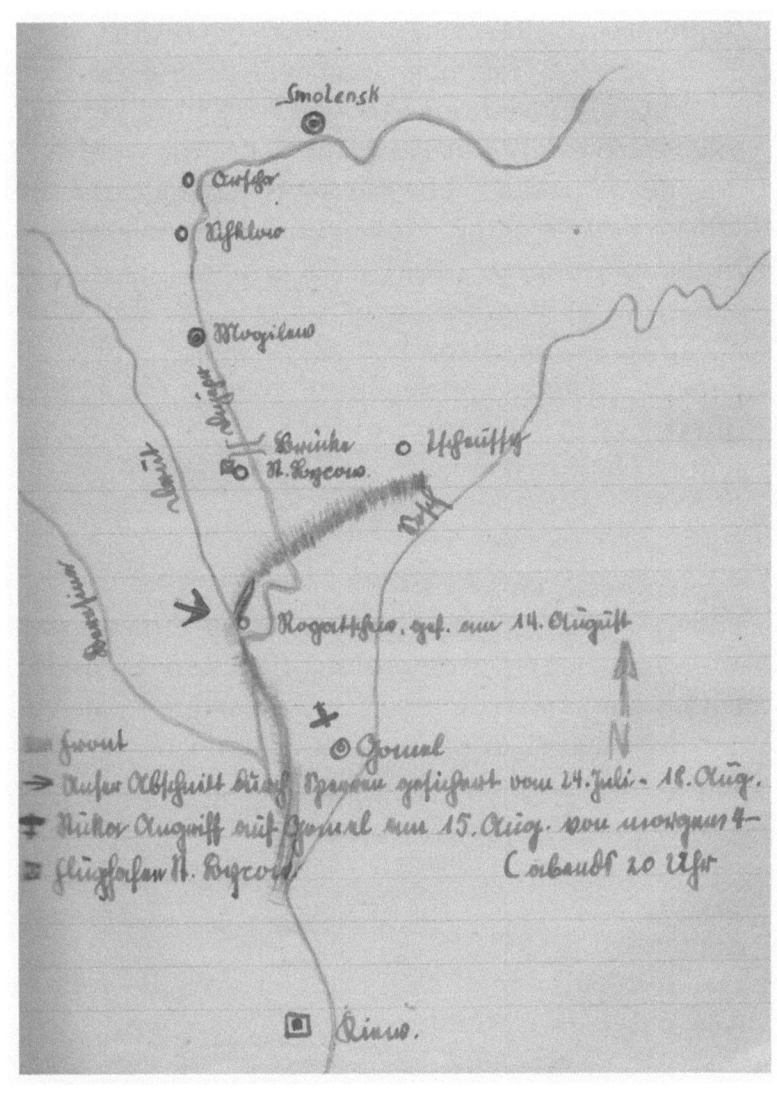

Handdrawn map,
in Pauls diary next to august 28th.

September 1, 1941
Two years of war, how long will it last? At 12.00 tonight we moved out. About 13 km from here is a village, taken by our company. The trip went well despite bad roads. The Russians have cleared the village early enough. However, artillery shot at us. In the morning we could see the silver glittering of some Soviet bombers over us. A few kilometers ahead of us they drop bombs. As soon as they are gone, other ones appear. In the morning, they flew directly over our camp and fired at two of our men without hitting them.

September 2, 1941
Finally a day off. This morning I got three parcels and three letters from Mom, Elsa and Eichstädt. Father has not written yet, and I have not received any mail at all from him yet. There's no point in writing for Lippspringe. Sent 270 Reichsmark back home today.

September 3, 1941
Had to repair a makeshift bridge today. It's raining cats and dogs. Nothing new.

Eichstädt. The woman in the picture is always called „Eichstädt" and appears to be Paul's love.

September 4, 1941
I've washed my uniform and laundry today. In the evening we have to proceed. Our company must strengthen the front units. But soon we will be replaced again, as reinforcements from the 167th Div. approaches.

September 5, 1941
Today it has rained all day. You can't do anything outside. In the evening I wrote letters home and to Gerda Klever.

September 6, 1941
We were announced to be mustered today – with all our stuff on. But after our meal we headed back on the road. Again, enemy aircraft were up in the air.

September 7, 1941
Our new boss was wounded last night at the clearing site. This morning he decided to leave the company and was sent to the hospital. Two Soviet Bombers flew low level over our heads

September 8, 1941
Inspection at 14.00 o'clock – we were mustered with all our stuff on. Everything's okay. An enemy's bomber dropped eight bombs just a few hundred meters ahead of us, only two exploded.

September 9, 1941
Today's another inspection, with weapons. Everything's okay. A low level flying bomber approached but turned away. Russian aircraft are up in the air all the time.

September 10, 1941
As in the previous days, artillery activity. The Russians try to attack again and again. But they had to pull back every time, with great losses.

September 11, 1941
The regiment has intercepted a Russian intelligence that the Soviets will attack that night. Okay, they will receive a warm welcome.

September 12, 1941
Last night at midnight, the Soviets attacked with two companies. They were not noticed sooner than the Russians laid 20 m away from the German positions, because at that moment the fog was leaving. The artillery, which was promptly requested, shot their munitions. The Soviets dug in themselves. Today the Soviets were put under fire with hand grenades and mortar shells.

September 13, 1941
Today the two Russian companies have surrendered. But are there still two? Of these, fifteen men had escaped, and sixty men were captured. Of these 60 are again 13 men who were not wounded. The others of the two companies were killed and cover the battlefield.

September 14, 1941
Been out for more road construction today. Had to drive wood. Again the Russians attacked the whole front without being able to assert himself.

September 15, 1941
There is a lively artillery activity again. We have not noon yet. But I will write down a story which has taken place here.

It was several days ago, when a machine gun in the foremost position of a company of the I.R. 17. Got stuck and couldn't get back to work as supposed. The gun was brought back and was tested and shot by the responsible NCO for weapons and another man. The bursts of fire whizzed into a forest, and after a short time more than 60 Soviet soldiers with 6 machine guns ran from the woods and surrendered. A good catch for little effort.

After lunch we laid out mines. This afternoon we've been on the left wing of I.R. 17 and placed S. mines. For us guys from the cab I slaughtered two chickens.

PFC Paul Velte

September 16, 1941
We get to know that the meat bowl we're encircling is completely closed. Four 4 Soviet armies are said to be in there.

September 17, 1941
18 men from the 1st platoon must spread out on a violent reconnaissance together with our infantry. At 18.00 o'clock the attack is scheduled. Everything works like on the parade grounds. The attack leads us directly into the middle of the enemy lines.
24 prisoners are made and a "wooden S.M.G." is captured. Mail from Mom, and Daddy sent cigarettes from Lippspringe.

September 18, 1941
Another rainy day. Gun inspections were scheduled but were cancelled due to fog.

September 19, 1941
I have just received my mother's and father's mail from Sept. 5th. My cousin Friederich died in the south of Russia. One of many. But don't think about that – war isn't over yet. Breaking news: The ring east of Gomel has been closed since the 13th of Sept. This meat bowl is south of us. The battle of extermination in progress is - unstoppable.

September 20, 1941
I had to drive to the battalion with my truck. A distance of just 38 km. I needed 4 hours. An indescribable road. This morning, like last night, we had visitors: two Soviet aircraft. But well placed M.G. bursts of fire made them turn away.

September 21, 1941
Road construction again. But done by noon. Rumors say they take us out of Russia. What I would welcome very much. But this is an issue we shouldn't think about for the time being. As long as the action is still here in the East, we will stay here.

September 22, 1941
Nothing special today. Again, the Russian aircrafts showed up twice today. Some few kilometers from here they tried a low level attack. We welcomed them with 9 M.G. and they immediately turned away.

September 23, 1941
At 14.00 o'clock we will be mustered in gas mask and all "accessories". I remember the time before the Soviet campaign and think about how often we have practiced with the gas mask. Several times a week was appeal. Day-by-day raising and lowering the gas mask in 7 seconds. Had to work just like a rifle attack. And all because the Soviets have had the best-equipped army in the gas war. Thank God, poison gas has not been used yet. It's getting cooler every day, the wind whistles over the steppes, icy rain rattles down on us, but I am still healthy and well. I wrote home tonight.

September 24, 1941
Who describes our astonishment when we got up this morning and found everything frozen. Everything is white of hoarfrost. We have a clear sky. Shortly after 8 o'clock a Soviet aircraft tried to attack us low level. But our M.G. gunners were combat ready. Immediately the Russian pulled the aircraft high and disappeared in a zigzag. The fire the Russian sent us was unsuccessful. This afternoon muster in all leather goods. Everything okay.

September 25, 1941
Today, 11 o'clock, field muster. Everything went well. Again, lively artillery activity. Some villages were on fire again. Night by night the Russian headlights stand above Bryansk. A sign that our bombers attack the city.

September 26, 1941
After lunch, the 1st and 3rd platoons had to get ready. We left at 13.00 o'clock. On their way, the 3rd platoon was attacked again and drove back. We headed towards the battalion. At the regimental command post of I.R 82 we suddenly got artillery fire. Apparently, the Russians had heard or seen us, for they shot pretty well. However, we came happy through the enemy's fire. We got our orders from the battalion. We drove 3 km further to the next village, which will be cleared tomorrow morning by the Brinkmann abbot. The regiment will move to this place tomorrow and we stay here to protect our commander. We sleep and live here in houses, which seem to be clean.

September 27, 1941
This morning we settled ourselves homely. A warm room after a long time. In the stable are more than 30 chickens. Let's see if they produce eggs. If not, we take the neck off and put them into the pot. Tonight our group had 7 chickens anyway. Tasted great. The purpose of our being here: First of all: protection of the commander of our battalion, then day and night watch for group 1 and 2. The following order is for the 3rd group. Every second night reconnaissance trips to the next village. 3 km. Every morning searching for mines from here to the next village, which is located 15 km away, because mines are often laid out during the night by palisades (Russian freighters). And finally, earning potatoes for the battalion. During this day many artillerymen and the construction battalion 157 arrived here. According to special reports, the fights in the Kiev are over. The booty of war material is unmistakable. Well, hopefully this place will be cleared out next. Yesterday evening at I.R. 82 as many as 600 men overrun. According to the prisoners, an unprecedented state is to prevail among the Soviets. Commissioners and officers are already shooting each other. Really Bolshevik attitude. At the moment the first drop of alcohol passes my lips. We also got cigarettes today. All post exchange goods.

September 28, 1941

At 5 o'clock this morning we started. The route to Kletnja must be searched for mines. As I wrote the route is 15 km. We came through without any disturbance. The Kletnja is a train station. We are astonished at the features which are already here. Indescribably how many troops are found here on their way to the front. A motorcyclist who drove right behind us got fired upon the forest. However, our return trip was without any incident. The whole way went through dense forest. - Today the third platoon has arrived. Tomorrow the whole company will come. New troops arrive every day. It will not be long and the attack will go up. The 31st Div. will be contracted. There are rumors running around, one as crazy as the other. Tomorrow we have to return to Kletnja. Hopefully this will work again.

These words are the last words PFC Paul Velte wrote. The following lines were written by his group leader, Sergeant Viktor Stephan:

This evening group III. is on guard
*　　　　　　　　　　　　　Stephan, Sgt.*

29.9.41 "no special incidents"

In the field 30.9.41
Group III. returned from guard at 5:00 o'clock. Had to mount the snow chains on the truck. Departure at 6 ½ o'clock. One of the worst roads ever. Dense forest and paths full of morass. Specific incidents: none.

In the field 1.10.41
All quiet. No special incidents.

*　　　　　　　　　　　　　　　　　In the field 2.10. 41*
3 ½ o'clock they woke up the company. 4 ¾ o'clock departure of the company (1st and 3rd platoon). On the wide horizon the sun blazes down on us. It is the perfect weather for the attack. I'm sitting in the cab. On the left is Paul, my driver, on the right is Anton Pochmann, my passenger. Paul and Anton are already smoking cigarettes, I myself my halfsize-pipe. Paul and Anton just

gave me their ration of cigars in exchange for my cigarettes. –On our way to the front line we were in a great mood. We remembered the time when we were resting in Bottrop (after the Poland campaign).

In the hollow paths and canyons, through which our path leads, more than batteries artillery are in position. Just to look at those powerful weapons made our mood even better.

In a meadow with marshy ground, all the vehicles got stuck. With great circumspection and tactics we got our truck out again. At this time, the enemy's artillery already shoots into the village near us, where our third platoon is waiting. Having arrived in this village, we stopped for a little while and our 1st platoon received the order to proceed to the next village and to build a road improved by wood sticks and mats of through the swampy terrain. The houses around were used for material procurement. When we started to work, our vehicles were about 150 meters away from our construction site. The roof of the first house was down, as the Russian artillery began to shoot. After several hits, a grenade hit the left corner of the house.

The three men standing on the top jumped down. Two meters apart was an infantryman on the ground who was easily wounded. A corporal from my group was badly wounded at the head and back, when we wanted to safe the infantry man's steel helmet. It was Corporal Werner Rödig. After three further hits in the immediate vicinity, the fire ceased.

After the injured were rescued and moved away with our platoon truck, the first platoon went back to work. About an hour later a new motorized unit arrived in our village. Thereupon the Russian artillery shot down the whole village. We tried to take cover.

So far, Paul would have been able to write.

The reports from 29.9.41 to 2.10.41 have been written down by me.
In the field, 5 October 1941

Viktor Stephan
         Sergeant

24 year old Paul Velte died on oct 2nd, 1941 when his lungs burst caused by the pressure wave of an exploding grenade.

Thoughts about the campaign against Russia

Paul wrote down his diary pertinaciously. When he started, he flipped his notebook open to some page in the last third of the book, never expecting to get that far.

Starting there, he wrote down his very own point of view about the war and the campaign against Russia.

You'll find a very different style of writing. That young man now appears very grown up and serious. Does this war make sense at all? What role is Germany playing in the world? What do they all expect from this war?

Remember – Paul could use only the information he had available. There was no world wide web, cell phone or newspaper – just what the Nazis provided: propaganda material.

But, regarding this, he did a great job to filter out what plain propaganda was and what they all believed this war was for.

The diary was filled day by day, page by page, and he came to the pages he had already filled. So Paul had to skip these pages and continue after his extra chapter. He numbered the pages, skipped that chapter and continued.

Editing this book, I decided to put the extra chapter at the end of this book to keep the diary independently.

Thoughts about the campaign against Russia
How often have we been thinking about the sense of the Eastern campaign. Yes, the German army is accustomed to fighting, is warlike. Who of us has not already participated in the Polish and Western campaign. Many were in Norway, in Greece and Serbia, that all are names which have entered the history of the world with an iron fist.

Perhaps the peculiar, unique aspect of the Soviet campaign, in which the middle we now are, becomes particularly clear to us. How often do you hear when comrades sit together in the evening: "How different was it in Belgium in France, or even in the sand deserts of Poland!"

How difficult it is to explain to our folks back home how the gloom of the Soviet world affects us soldiers. How often ridiculous the Soviet system affects our simplest living habits. You'll regret, if – and that can easily happen when you break a crest or a mirror, even the good piece of furniture is irreplaceable in the whole Soviet Union. So is the situation with many things that we need for daily use. And the reason for this is probably because the Soviet system was in no way compatible with the distribution of goods. Occasionally in smaller cities, but then in senseless accumulation, they have this single article. So I remember a shop of Kolekos, of which I wrote many times, where they had shaving brushes of the cheapest quality on the one hand and toothbrushes on the other hand - the purest scrap. Perhaps one day we will come to a city where we can probably replace our broken mirror or something else

But in libraries, there are heaps of pictures of Lenin and Stalin. In addition, manuals on the tactics of air warfare and tank guns.

But when will we arrive in a real city? I have driven 2,300 km through the Soviet Russian country so far. This endless country sucks us up. And despite the bright colors of the late summer, and although there are also cornflowers, poppies and sunflowers, everything appears to us in the same tint, wrapped in the silence of the steppe. Everything is gray in gray. Often we see a beautiful terrain. In front of us is a desolate marsh landscape, with its high reed grass and dense opaque alder trees. On the horizon you can see the silhouette of a typical Russian peasant village. To the left and right of the village are draw-fountains, which we can imagine any longer. And yet the landscape is dull and cloudy.

The uniform system of colchos has led to gigantic monolithic cultivation surfaces, to entire stretches of land forming only a single contiguous cornfield, or a single potato harvester, or a huge wheat surface. This is interrupted by the never-ending sand fields, or by the huge forests of White Russia. Virgin forests, whose green twilight probably contains wolves, perhaps even bears. We do not know, because when we go through them, we have to pay attention to other things. Between the woods are villages, always same looking villages. One or two ancient draw-fountains, which stretch their wooden arms like an oath against the heavens. A little off the banja or sauna, steam bathes imported from Finland to Russia. And then the wooden huts, if these are worth that name, with straw roofs, gray, bent by age.

When we pitch our tent camp in such a village, it is like an island from another world, a clear, richer, and much more awake world. Every German soldier is here as a Robinson, a lonely civilized man in the wilderness, in these plains, swamps and forests. And like Robinson, he has to assert himself, day by day he must create a new world in the dull villages out of the desolation.

May never lose his courage, lose his joyful being. What a glorious attitude these men show, whose laughter and humor come out at dawn as if it wakes up this whole country. For this country has not awakened yet, and its people here in the villages sometimes appear to us like cattle, crowded spilling out the front doors.

"Soviet Union children's paradise", that's what they named it. A free paradise. Russia has over 30 million children, about half of these 30 million have learned to write and read. The other half is systematically brought up as criminals or hobos. Early they are expelled from their wretched mothers, wandering through the country, weird, neglected. And despite their youth, they do not shy away from theft or even murder. Many are taken up and come to children's homes or correctional facilities. Does the child find a home here? How could it. Let us look at the homes. Poor wooden barracks, linger to the highest degree, and the educators? Are not they themselves criminals? Criminals at the youth. "Kids paradise!"

But we are here because of the war, a war that shows such a peculiar and ambiguous face! This harsh war, so hopeless for the Soviets. With what intensity they had prepared themselves. How they had tried to draw all the lessons from the German campaigns, these our most attentive pupils. The high number of their destroyed tanks and airplanes give an illuminating picture of the technical progress of their army. For a long time, their tractor factories had switched to tank production. Numerous artillery, motorized divisions Pak and Flak - they had everything.

How they have been rushing to war for months, making Moscow the center and the stone heart of their overorganization. They raised "Heil Moskau" to the battle slogan of the international class struggle. They must also face war against Moscow, and throw their entire wealth of people and material against Moscow.

In huge tension the German tanks smashed their front into large parts. Then they tried to form three army groups under Waroshilov, Tymoshenko, and Budjenny. The English radio station talks the same trash as the Soviets do, that the Bolshevik front has remained the inner mobility which is so necessary for them.

But at that moment, the warfare of the Red Army had lost its inner connection. And the takeover of Stalin's command was only political and propagandistic.

One thing, however, has to be emphasized, which has also been said repeatedly by the reports of the Wehrmacht and the rapporteurs: "The single Bolshevik soldier proved to be a very tenacious and obstinate opponent." Two reasons therefore seem to be decisive.

The stubborn, often Mongolian and Cartesian human material obeyed blindly the commands of the commissaries and commanders.

Dumb, crowded in dense heaps, they ran into the bursts of fire of the German machine guns. The other reason was the incitement of the Russian soldier, who was fundamentally convinced that he would be murdered after being captured by cruel torture.

The cowardly war behind the front gave hard times to the German soldier. As often, scattered Bolshevik troops, who sought shelter in the vast forests of Russia, came out of the darkness to attack German convoys.

Supply convoys often suffered heavy losses. With all the indifference of an Asian, they attacked us, and then tried to disappear under the cover of the vast forests. It is only after the capture that one sees fear about the upcoming in their faces. The first thing they did, however, was that they tore the Soviet stars and rank-badges from their uniforms, so they trotted along like a dull mass, escaped the murderous compulsion of their commissaries.

"How often the German army and leadership has passed huge stress tests. As they proved themselves that they will belong to the eternal glorious epitaph of German history !"

In the field, september 10, 1941

Notifications to Pauls familiy

When a soldier died, the unit took care of his belongings and managed notifications and condolences to the family – at least in this early phase of WW II.

The company commander as well as comrades wrote letters – handwritten or with typewriter. All belongings - from socks to chewing gum and cigarettes – were listed and sent back home.

Even photos of the grave were taken – in a time, when photography was expensive and complicated to handle!

On the following pages you'll find a selection of scans of the original letters, list etc. which show how the family was notified and how comrades as well as authorities took care about the loss.

In the field, 3.X.41

Dear valued Velte family !

As company commander I have the painful task to tell you about the heroic death of your son.

On the 2.X., the day of the beginning of the new East campaign, the company had orders to build a bridge in the front line over the Roscha brook, about 50 km west of Briansk. Although the enemy still had the village one kilometer above the stream in his hands and could see the bridge, the bridge had to be built to ensure the most important success of the regiment. Around noon, at 13:00 o'clock, the Russian surprised us with heavy artillery fire raids of the heaviest caliber, in which we lost a comrade by severe injury. At 16.00 o'clock the enemy repeated the same fire attack. Your son had jumped into a bunker with four other comrades and had found cover under a 50 cm thick layer of soil. There could be no better protection in the wider environment. By chance, however, a bouncer hit this bunker, causing your son to be buried and dead.

He had a slight injury only on his head. In the village Wyssokoje he found his last retirement.

Be assured that I feel your pain with you. We lost in your son a comrade, who had grown heartfelt to all company members. By his calm, modest nature, by his servant and his sense of duty, he had acquired the full affection of all his comrades and superiors. We lose in him one of the best. He gave his young life for leaders, people and fatherland, for his homeland, which he could not see again.

> I would like to express my sincere condolences to you on behalf of the Company
>
> Ernst Drinkut
> Lieutenant and Company commander

In the field, oct. 17, 1941

Valued Velte family !

As Sergeant and group leader I want to write some lines to the relatives of my driver Paul, to the loss, which concerns all of us.

I myself joined the 3rd Mt. Pl. 31 together with your son Paul on sep 17, 1938 in Höxter. I participated in the Poland campaign and the West campaign as a pioneer and corporal. I was a gunner in both campaigns. Your son Paul was already during peace times the driver of our group truck. Since I have committed myself for a longer period of service, I have been promoted to sergeant in November. Then I became group leader of the third group and got the truck that Paul drove.

When this campaign began, Paul and I become quite good comrades for a long time. I was glad to have Paul as my driver. We met first, when the Polish campaign was over and we were in Bottrop. We often went out together, namely Paul, Joseph Kuhlmann, who got wounded and now lies in Johannisburg / East Prussia and I. I became the third member of the team.

I express my condolences to you to the loss of your son and brother.

I do not know if there is any consolation, it is just the condolences of a frontal soldier. I know what loss and consolation is. The fights are not over yet and we still have to fight with the Bolsheviks. Who will it be tomorrow?

There is not much to tell about Paul's death. Paul was immediately killed in the attack. There was therefore no thought between impact and death. All my comrades and I cannot believe that Paul was torn out of our midst.

Paul was always helpful and always a comrade in every respect. I could always rely on Paul. I could never complain. A noble character, clean and good. Jokingly, we called Paul VA (catering office). Paul, our co-driver Anton Pochmann and I always ate our food together, Paul managed everything.

When it all was over, tears were in our eyes.
His sacrifice is a legacy to all of us.

The Lord may give the eternal rest to our brave Paul

Greetings to you even unknown
        The comrades of the third group
        and Sergeant Viktor Stephan

Nachlasssachen des O. Gefr. **V e l t e !**

durch die Post an Ihre Adresse:

- 1 Traeningsanzug
- 1 Badeanzug
- 1 Wollpullover
- 1 Pr. Handschuhe
- 1 Pr. Struempfe
- 14 Taschentuecher
- 1 Kleiderbuerste
- 1 Turnhose
- 1 buntes Hemd
- 1 Pfeife
- 1 Armbanduhr
- 1 Fahrtenmesser mit Etui
- 18 Rasierklingen
- 100 Zigaretten
- 1 Zigarettenetui
- 1 Nagelscheere
- 1 Minenetui fuer Blei
- 3 Rollen Pfefferminz
- 1 Dose Nivea Hautcreme
- 1 Taschenlampe
- 1 Mappe mit Schreibsachen Tagebuch, Briefe, Aufnahmen
- 1 Etui mit Naehnadeln
- 1 Etui mit Fueller und Zigarettenspitze

Im Felde, den 17. Oktober 1941

J Uhl
Leutnant u. Komp.-Chef

Opposite page:

<u>Belongings of PFC V e l t e !</u>
via mail to your address:

1	Sports suit
1	Bathing suit
1	Sweater
1	Pr. Gloves
1	Pr. socks
14	handkerchiefs
1	Clothing brush
1	Sports shorts
1	Colorful shirt
1	Pipe
1	Watch
1	Knife with holster
18	razor blades
100	Cigarettes
1	Cigarette case
1	Nail clipper
1	Mines case for pencils
3	Rolls of peppermint
1	Can Nivea creme
1	Flashlight
1	Folder with writing supplies Diary, letters, Photos
1	Case with sewing needles
1	Case with ink pen and cigarette tip

Nach bangen Tagen der Ungewißheit erhielten wir heute von seinem Kompanieführer die Nachricht, daß am 2. Oktober 1941, bei den Kämpfen bei Briansk unser einziger, geliebter Sohn, mein guter Bruder und Kamerad, unser lieber Neffe und Vetter, unser Junior-Chef

Paul Velte
Obergefreiter in einem Pionier-Batl.

kurz vor seinem 25. Geburtstage sein Leben für Führer, Volk und Vaterland hingegeben hat.

In tiefem Schmerz:

Paul Velte und Frau, Else geb. Jäger
Elsa Velte
und Anverwandte,

Betriebsführer und Gefolgschaft
der Firma **Gebr. Velte**.

Remscheid-Hasten, Köln, den 28. Oktober 1941.
Ludendorffstr. 34

Death notice in local newspaper

Der Kreisleiter   Remscheid-Lennep, 3. Januar 1942
Kreis Bergisch-Land

Sehr geehrte Familie Velte !

Durch den derzeitigen Leiter der Ortsgruppe Remscheid-Hasten, Parteigenossen Schwabeland, erfahre ich von dem schweren Verlust, der Sie durch den Tod Ihres Sohnes betroffen hat.

Es ist schwer, in einem solchen Falle ein tröstendes inneres Mitfühlen zum Ausdruck zu bringen, denn Worte sind nichts, können niemals die Lücke schließen, die das Opfer, das Sie für uns alle bringen mussten, gerissen hat.

Doch möchte ich Sie meiner Verbundenheit versichern im Gedenken an Ihren Sohn, der gegen den Feind aller Zivilisation und Kultur, gegen den Bolschewismus, der brutal und rücksichtslos jedes Familienleben und jede menschliche Lebensfreiheit zu vernichten drohte, so mutig gekämpft und durch seinen Soldatentod seinen Eid auf den Führer und für Grossdeutschland erfüllt hat.

Gestatten Sie mir deshalb diese Zeilen.
Können sie Ihnen nicht Trost sein, so mögen
sie Ihnen Kraft geben aus der Erkenntnis,
dass auch dieses Opfer nicht umsonst gebracht
wurde für die Zukunft unseres Volkes und den
Frieden unserer Kinder und Kindeskinder.

Heil Hitler !

Ihr

Letter on previous pages:

Der Kreisleiter   Remscheid-Lennep, Jan. 3, 1942
Kreis Bergisch-Land

Dear Velte family!

Informed by the leader of the local group Remscheid-Hasten, party comrade Schwabeland, I've learned about the heavy loss you've experienced by the death of your son.

In such case it is difficult to express consolatory feelings, because words are nothing, can never close the gap that the casualty you have has left open.

But I would like to assure you of my loyalty to your son, who fought so courageously against the enemy of all civilization and culture, against Bolshevism, who brutally and recklessly threatened to destroy every family life and every human freedom of life, and fulfilled with his soldier's death his oath on the Führer and for Great Germany

Therefore, allow me these lines. They might be no consolation, but they might give you power knowing that this death wasn't senseless but for the future of our children and grandchildren.

                        Heil Hitler!

                        Yours
                        (Signature)

Wehrmeldeamt Remscheid
Sachgeb.Res. -o- /42   Remscheid, 3. März 1942

Am 2. Oktober 1941 starb der
Obergefreite
Paul　V e l t e
Remscheid, Ludendorffstrasse 34
den Heldentod für Führer, Volk und
Vaterland.

Als früherer Wehrpflichtiger des Beurlaubtenstandes
unterstand der Gefallene dem Wehrmeldeamt Remscheid.

Bestimmungsgemäss verbleibt der Jahrpass der Gefallenen
als letzte Erinnerung im Besitz der nächsten Angehörigen.

                                    Major und Leiter
                                    des Wehrmeldeamtes

Herrn
Paul　V e l t e
R e m s c h e i d.
Ludendorffstrasse 34

-1- Wehrpass

Opposite Page:

Wehrmeldeamt Remscheid   Remscheid, March 3, 1942
Sachgeb.Res. -o-/42

On October 2., 1941
PFC
Paul V e l t e
Remscheid, Ludendorffstrasse 34
died a hero's death for Führer, nation and his homeland.

As previous conscript the fallen was supervised by Wehrmeldeamt Remscheid

According to our regulations you receive the military ID of your loss as a last memory.

(Signature)
Major and leader
of the Wehrmeldeamt

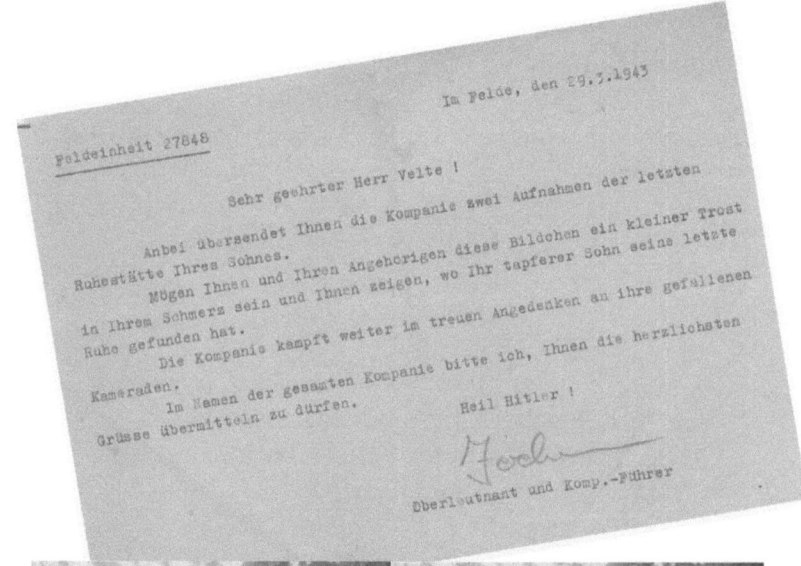

Paul's last rest

Opposite page:

Outpost 27848   In the field, march 3, 1943

Dear Mr. Velte!

with this letter you'll receive two photos taken from the last rest of your son.
These photos might be some consolation in your pain and show you, where your brave son found his last rest. The company keeps fighting, always thinking about their fallen comrades.
In the name of the whole company I kindly ask you to accept our wishes.

Heil Hitler !
(Signature)
Captain and company commander

Einheit Im Felde, den 22.12.43
der Feldpostnr. 27948

Sehr geehrte Familie Velte

Angesichts des dicht bevorstehenden Weihnachtsfestes und
des nahenden Jahreswechsels möchte es die Kompanie nicht ver-
säumen Ihnen, Herr Velte die herzlichsten Grü-
ße und Wünsche für diese beiden Feste zu übermitteln. Die ganze Kompanie denkt in diesen Tagen an Ihre Kameraden, die uns
auf diese schmerzliche Art mit Weiss verlassen mußten. Noch
oft sitzen wir alle zusammen und reden von den gemeinsam ver-
lebten frohen und schlechten Stunden. Dabei denken wir besonders
an Sie, warter Herr Velte und wie schmerzlich Sie von
der Verluste Ihres Sohnes betroffen worden sind.
Aber es ist ja ein großer Trost zu wissen, daß Ihr Sohn
nicht umsonst gefallen ist, sondern für eine große Sache:" für
die Zukunft Deutschlands." Wie es in dem Buch " Mein Kampf"
geschrieben steht: Sie mußten sterben, damit wir leben können!
Warter Herr Velte , lassen Sie den Mut nicht sinken, und
sind Sie stolz darauf, daß Ihr Sohn das Höchste was er
besaß, sein Leben, für das Bestehen Groß-Deutschlands geben
konnte. Wir alle sind stolz auf ihn, denn er ist ein Held ge-
wesen!

Die ganze Kompanie grüßt Sie nun herzlichst und wünscht
Ihnen zu beiden Festen alles Gute und Schöne, und mögen sich
Ihre traurigen Gedanken in starke und zuversichtlich in die
Zukunft schauende Wünsche und Hoffnungen verwandeln. Wir alle
wollen Sie darin unterstützen.
Ich grüße Sie herzlichst und mit

Heil Hitler

Hauptmann u. Kp.-Chef

Opposite page:

Unit of outpostNo 27848   In the field, dec. 22, 1943

Dear Velte family !

Regarding the upcoming xmas celebrations and the new year our company will not forget to wish you, Mr. Velte, all the best.
The whole company thinks about their comrades, who had to leave us in such a terrible way
We often sit together and talk about the good times and the bad times we've spent together. Mr. Velte, we especially think of you and how hard you were hit by the loss of your son.
But it is a consolation to know, that your son hasn't died without sense but for the great task: for Germany's future. Like in the book "Mein Kampf" is written: they had to die so that we can live!
Dear Mr. Velte, don't drop your courage and be proud that your son could give his life, the best he could give for the existence of Great Germany. We are all proud of him, because he was a hero!
The whole company salutes and wishes all the best to you and your family, may your sad thoughts get strong and confident. We all will assist you,
 Best wishes and
  Heil Hitler !
  (Signature)
 Captain and company commander

Acronyms and Abbreviations

Paul used different abbreviations and terms. These are explained below.
These abbreviations and terms do not always correspond to todays state or understanding.

Btl.	Bataillon	Batallion
Div.	Division	Division
E.K.2	Eisernes Kreuz II	Iron Cross 2 = WW II medal
Flak	Flugabwehrkanone	Air defence gun
Gefr	Gefreiter	Corporal
Hbh	Hauptbahnhof	Main station, railway station
Inf.	Infanterie	Infantry
IR	Infanterieregiment	Infantry regiment
MG	Maschinengewehr	Machine gun
Oberleutn.	Oberleutnant	1st Lieutenant
OGefr	Obergefreiter	Private first class
PAK	Panzerabwehrkanone	Anti tank gun
Pi	Pionier	Pioneer
RM	Reichsmark	Reichsmark (currency)
S-Mine	Schrapnellmine	antipersonnel mine
T-Mine	Tellermine	antitank mine
Uffz	Unteroffizier	Sergeant

Names and Persons

Paul mentioned different (in)famous persons in his diary. As a quick reference some short biographies are added. All biographies taken from Wikipedia and edited (shortened) by the author.

Werner Mölders

(18 March 1913 – 22 November 1941) was a World War II German Luftwaffe pilot and the leading German fighter ace in the Spanish Civil War. Mölders became the first pilot in aviation history to claim 100 aerial victories—that is, 100 aerial combat encounters resulting in the destruction of the enemy aircraft, and was highly decorated for his achievements. He was instrumental in the development of new fighter tactics that led to the finger-four formation. He died in an air crash in which he was a passenger.

Mölders joined the Luftwaffe in 1934 at the age of 21. In 1938, he volunteered for service in the Condor Legion, which supported General Francisco Franco's Nationalist side in the Spanish Civil War, and shot down 14 aircraft. In World War II, he lost two wingmen in the Battle of France and the Battle of Britain, but shot down 53 enemy aircraft. With his tally standing at 68 victories, Mölders and his unit, the Jagdgeschwader 51 (JG 51), were transferred to the Eastern Front in June 1941 for the opening of Operation Barbarossa.

By the end of 22 June 1941, the first day of Barbarossa, he had added another four victories to his tally and a week later, Mölders surpassed Manfred von Richthofen's 1918 record of 80 victories. By mid-July, he had 100 World War II victories.

Paul Joseph Goebbels

(29 October 1897 – 1 May 1945) was a German politician and Reich Minister of Propaganda of Nazi Germany from 1933 to 1945. He was one of Adolf Hitler's close associates and most devoted followers, and was known for his skills in public speaking and his deep, virulent antisemitism, which was evident in his publicly voiced views. He advocated progressively harsher discrimination, including the extermination of the Jews in the Holocaust.

Ulrich Friedrich Wilhelm Joachim von Ribbentrop

(30 April 1893 – 16 October 1946), more commonly known as Joachim von Ribbentrop, was Foreign Minister of Nazi Germany from 1938 until 1945.

Ribbentrop first came to Adolf Hitler's notice as a well-travelled businessman with more knowledge of the outside world than most senior Nazis and as an authority on world affairs. He offered his house for the secret meetings in January 1933 that resulted in Hitler's appointment as Chancellor of Germany. He became a close confidant of Adolf Hitler, to the disgust of some party members, who thought him superficial and lacking in talent. He was nevertheless appointed Ambassador to the Court of St James (for the United Kingdom of Great Britain and Northern Ireland) in 1936 and then Foreign Minister of Germany in February 1938.

Before World War II, he played a key role in brokering the Pact of Steel (an alliance with fascist Italy) and the Nazi–Soviet non-aggression pact, known as the Molotov–Ribbentrop Pact. After 1941, Ribbentrop's influence declined.

Arrested in June 1945, Ribbentrop was tried at the Nuremberg trials and convicted for his role in starting World War II and enabling the Holocaust. On 16 October 1946, he became the first of those sentenced to death to be hanged.